To Eddy Spaghetti Rabe and to the PAWS
(Pet Animal Welfare Society) Shelter of
Norwalk, Connecticut, for helping us make
him a beloved member of our family
—T.R.

The editors would like to thank
BARBARA KIEFER, Ph.D.,
Charlotte S. Huck Professor of Children's Literature,
The Ohio State University, and
STEPHEN L. ZAWISTOWSKI, Ph.D., CAAB,
Adjunct Professor of Clinical Medicine,
University of Illinois College of Veterinary Medicine,
for their assistance in the preparation of this book.

All rights reserved. Published in the United States by Random House Children's Books,
a division of Random House, Inc., New York.

Random House and the colophon are registered trademarks of Random House, Inc.

Visit us on the Web!
randomhouse.com/kids
Seussville.com

Educators and librarians, for a variety of teaching tools, visit us at
RHTeachersLibrarians.com

Library of Congress Cataloging-in-Publication Data
Rabe, Tish.
What cat is that? : all about cats / by Tish Rabe ; illustrated by Aristides Ruiz and
Joe Mathieu. — First edition.
    pages cm. — (The cat in the hat's learning library)
Audience: 5–8.
Summary: "The Cat in the Hat learns all about cats—wild and domestic—in this feline-focused
Cat in the Hat's Learning Library book." — Provided by publisher.
ISBN 978-0-375-86640-1 (trade) — ISBN 978-0-375-96640-8 (lib. bdg.)
1. Cats—Juvenile literature. I. Ruiz, Aristides, illustrator. II. Mathieu, Joe, 1949– illustrator.
III. Title.
QL737.C23R245 2013 599.75—dc23 2013002984

Printed in the United States of America 10 9 8 7 6 5 4 3 2 1 First Edition

Cat Is That?

by Tish Rabe

illustrated by Aristides Ruiz and Joe Mathieu

The Cat in the Hat's Learning Library®

Random House 🏠 New York

I'm the Cat in the Hat.
Let us leave right away
to see all the cats
we can see in one day.

We'll meet lions in Kenya,
tigers in Bangkok,
snow leopards in China,
Siamese down the block.

In my Kitty-Cat-Copter
we'll travel around
to all different places
where cats can be found!

Cats are mammals that have
scratchy tongues, padded paws,
sensitive whiskers,
and very sharp claws.

Cats like to chase,
pounce, eat, wrestle, and hide.
Some cats live indoors.
Some cats live outside.

Here's a fact about cats
I did not know before:
Some can roar but can't purr.
Some can purr but can't roar!

Tigers are the biggest.
They hunt in the night.
Most are orange with black stripes
and patches of white.

Ocelots, like this one,
are cats that are rare.
Go to a rain forest.
You might find one there.

Leopards are strong, and as you can see, a leopard can quickly climb up a tree.

Some cats are wild,
like the ones we just met.
A domesticated cat
can be kept as a pet.

Persians have long fur,
and I'd like to mention,
their long, silky coats
need a lot of attention.

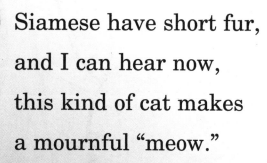

Siamese have short fur,
and I can hear now,
this kind of cat makes
a mournful "meow."

Do cats like to swim?
You may think "No way,"
but Turkish swimming cats
like to get wet and play!

Cats need to scratch
to take care of their paws.
When they scratch, they are pulling
dead skin off their claws.

SNOW LEOPARD

Cats' claws are strong.
Here's another cat fact:
Cats' claws can extend.
They can also retract.

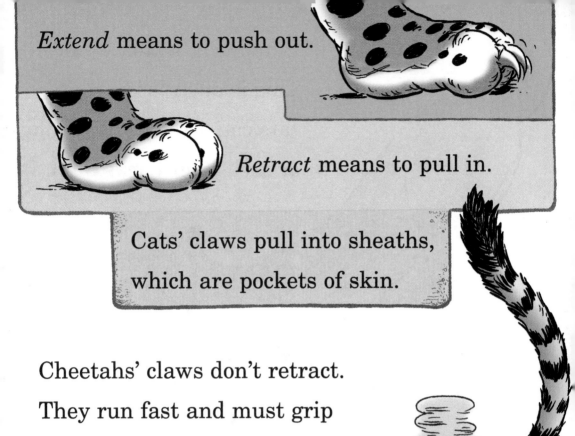

Extend means to push out.

Retract means to pull in.

Cats' claws pull into sheaths, which are pockets of skin.

Cheetahs' claws don't retract.
They run fast and must grip
the ground with their claws
so their paws will not slip.

COUGAR

Cats have flexible spines. This is one reason why cats can stretch really long or arch their backs high.

Cats have small collarbones, which can move so cats fit through small spaces, like doors opened up just a bit.

Cats' rear legs are strong
and that's what they need.
To catch food they must run
with strength and with speed.

SERVAL

Cats need their whiskers
and use them each day.
Like your fingertips, whiskers
help cats find their way.

Whiskers help cats
know which way they are going,
if it's cold out or hot,
and which way the wind's blowing.

OCELOT

Cats use their whiskers
each time they explore.

"Is this hard, smooth, or rough?"

"Can I fit through this door?"

Cats can have different markings—
stripes, patches, or spots.
Some cats have few markings
and others have lots.

This tiger has black stripes,
an orange-red coat,
white fur on its belly,
chest, muzzle, and throat.

This cat is white with colored patches, and that is how I know she is a calico cat.

This clouded leopard told me she is proud that each of her spots looks a bit like a cloud.

Cats are active at dawn
and again at twilight.
For this reason, they see
very well in dim light.

In dim light, cats' pupils
grow round and wide.
This lets their eyes get
the most light inside.

Look at a cat's eyes
when the light is bright.
Its pupils get narrow
so they let in less light.

MARGAY

Cells in back of their eyes
reflect light, and so
a cat's eyes at night
let off a bright glow!

Cats have different ears.
A Scottish fold cat
has ears that can bend
and are folded and flat.

CARACAL

SAND CAT

I just met these cats—
a boy and a girl.
They're American curl cats
and their ears can curl.

When a cat hears a noise,
its ears turn around,
so each ear can focus
on one single sound.

A cat's nose is wet, and here's one reason why— it picks up smells better than one that is dry.

Cats are carnivores, which means they eat meat.

They taste sour, bitter, and salty but cannot taste sweet.

Cats have sharp teeth
to tear meat and bite.
Some use their teeth
when they get in a fight.

BOBCATS

When a cat is upset,
it might roar or growl.
When a cat is angry,
it might start to howl.

When a cat is threatened,
it might act like this—
it arches its back
and lets out a loud hiss.

A dog wags its tail
when it's excited or glad.
A cat twitches its tail
when it's nervous or mad.

Thing One looked up cat words
and here is the scoop:
What is a clowder?
It's cats in a group!

When cats rub their cheeks, they leave scent on each other. This tiger cub's leaving her scent on her mother.

This lion is rubbing a tree with his face. His scent tells other cats, "I have been at this place."

When a cat starts to circle
and bumps into you,
leaving its scent,
as Tarzee likes to do . . .

this is called "bunting."
Cats do this, you see,
as their way of saying
"You belong to me."

Cats don't bathe or shower, but they have a trick. A cat takes a front paw and gives it a lick.

It sweeps the wet paw over its head, and then it takes the same paw and licks it again.

Spines on a cat's tongue
help it work like a scraper.
They're rough, and they make
the tongue feel like sandpaper.

Thing Two has a new cat.
He's called Mr. Pickles.
When he licks you, his tongue
is so rough that it tickles!

When wild cats have babies,
mother cats stay alert
to make sure that their
little cubs don't get hurt.

Mother lion keeps her cubs
right by her side.
They blend in with the grass,
and that helps them to hide.

A tiger must raise
her cubs all alone.
In a few years her cubs
will go off on their own.

She licks her cubs
as a sign of affection.
It's her job to find food
and give them protection.

35

Now I would like
to take you to meet
a litter of kittens
that live down the street.

Born with no teeth
and with eyes that are blue,
these sweet little kittens
are glad to meet you.

Newborn kittens are helpless.
They depend on their mother.
In a few weeks they'll start
to play with each other.

What is a kindle?
Hold on to your socks.
It's a group of kittens,
like these in this box.

KINDLE

When a cat moves her baby,
she carefully holds
the skin on its neck
where it hangs in loose folds.

It won't hurt a kitty
to be moved by its mother
by the scruff of its neck
from one place to another.

Mountain lion and *cougar* are names for this cat. So are *puma* and *panther*. Now, how about that!

Kittens grow quickly and, as you see here, a kitten grows into a cat in one year.

Cats live just about
anywhere that you go—
cities, rain forests,
mountains covered in snow.

Cats like to sleep,
and most cats sleep a lot—
on the ground, in a tree,
in a warm, sunny spot.

So now I am sure
cats are taking a nap
all over the world
and right here . . .

. . . in your lap.

GLOSSARY

Calico: Having fur with multi-colored patches.

Collarbone: A curved bone that supports the shoulder.

Cubs: The young of certain animals, such as lions, tigers, and bears.

Domesticated: Tamed, meaning that an animal is comfortable with people and can't live in the wild.

Flexible: Bending easily.

Focus: To direct one's attention to a single thing.

Litter: A group of babies born at the same time to one mother.

Muzzle: The part of an animal's head that includes the mouth and nose.

Pounce: To swoop down on something suddenly.

Pupil: The black part in the center of the eye, which is a hole that lets in light.

Scruff: The back of the neck.

Threatened: In danger.

Twilight: The period of dim light before sunset.

FOR FURTHER READING

Big Cats by Seymour Simon (HarperCollins). Illustrated with photographs, this is an award-winning book about big wild cats—including lions, tigers, leopards, jaguars, cheetahs, pumas, and snow leopards. For ages 5–8.

Cats vs. Dogs by Elizabeth Carney (National Geographic *Kids Readers,* Level 3). A lively comparison of cats and dogs—their ancestors, senses, social lives, and more. For ages 6–8.

Discover Maine Coon Cats by Trudy Micco (Enslow Publishers, *Discover Cats with the Cat Fanciers' Association*). All about the history of Maine coon cats and how to care for them. Other books in the *Discover Cats* series are about Abyssinian, Oriental shorthair, Persian, ragdoll, and mixed-breed cats. For kindergarten–grade 3.

Learning to Care for a Cat by Felicia Lowenstein Niven (Enslow Publishers, *Beginning Pet Care with American Humane*). A simple guide to cat pet care, written with the help of an expert from the American Humane Association. For grades 3–4.

INDEX

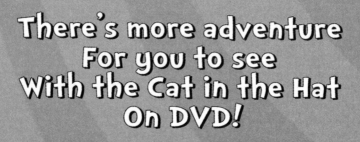